# SIR ALEX
# FERGUSON
## 1986–2013

# SIR ALEX FERGUSON

# 1986–2013

## THE GREATEST MANAGER IN HIS OWN WORDS

EBURY
PRESS

5 7 9 10 8 6 4

Published in 2013 by Ebury Press, an imprint of Ebury Publishing
A Random House Group company

The Random House Group Limited Reg. No. 954009

Addresses for companies within the Random House Group
can be found at www.randomhouse.co.uk

A CIP catalogue record for this book is available from the British Library

The Random House Group Limited supports the Forest Stewardship
Council® (FSC®), the leading international forest-certification
organisation. Our books carrying the FSC label are printed
on FSC®-certified paper. FSC is the only forest-certification
scheme supported by the leading environmental organisations, including
Greenpeace. Our paper procurement policy can be found at
www.randomhouse.co.uk/environment

Printed and bound by CPI Group (UK) Ltd, Croydon, CR0 4YY

ISBN 9780091957322

To buy books by your favourite authors and register for offers visit
www.randomhouse.co.uk

*With thanks to Mark Robins*

# NAYSAYERS
# UNITED

# 3 YEARS OF EXCUSES AND IT'S STILL CRAP, TA-RA FERGIE.

*Banner at Old Trafford, December 1989*

**WHAT REALLY HURTS, ALEX, IS THAT UNDER YOU WE'VE HAD SHIT FOOTBALL, SHIT ATMOSPHERE, SHIT BOARDROOM SHENANIGANS AND OUR SUPPORT IS DRIFTING AWAY.**

*Fanzine* Red News *editorial, December 1989*

# OBE –
# OUT BEFORE EASTER.

*Emlyn Hughes awards Sir Alex
an alternative honour, 1990*

# FERGIE, FERGIE,
# ON THE DOLE.

*Nottingham Forest fans during FA Cup
third round match, January 1990.
If Manchester United had lost, Sir Alex's job
was reportedly on the line. They won 1-0*

# LET'S NOT GET CARRIED AWAY. THE DAYS ARE OVER WHEN ONE CLUB CAN DOMINATE OUR GAME.

*George Graham, following
Alex Ferguson's first league title, 1993*

# YOU CAN'T WIN ANYTHING WITH KIDS ... THE TRICK ABOUT WINNING THE CHAMPIONSHIP IS TO HAVE STRENGTH IN DEPTH. THEY JUST HAVEN'T GOT IT.

Match of the Day*'s Alan Hansen on the new-look young Manchester United, 1995*

# THE DAY THAT FERGUSON'S EMPIRE BEGAN TO CRUMBLE

*Headline in* The Times, *after
United's 2001 defeat by Liverpool*

# BELIEFS

**I GREW UP IN A
VERY WORKING CLASS
AREA OF GLASGOW,
BELIEVING LABOUR
WAS THE PARTY OF THE
WORKING MAN, AND
I STILL BELIEVE THAT.**

*Sir Alex Ferguson, 2009*

# I THINK GLASWEIGANS, AND PEOPLE IN THE WEST OF SCOTLAND, GROW UP IN A DIFFERENT CLIMATE.

*Sir Alex Ferguson, 2008*

**THESE PEOPLE BUILT
THE BEST SHIPS IN THE
WORLD. YOU CAN OVER-
ROMANTICISE THESE
THINGS, BUT THEY DO
HAVE A REAL PART TO
PLAY IN FORGING A
PERSON'S CHARACTER.**

*Sir Alex Ferguson on working
in Fraserburgh, 2008*

IT'S TRUE I'VE EARNED
A LOT OF MONEY. BUT
I'VE WORKED HARD,
PAID MY TAXES AND
PUT A LOT BACK IN
DIFFERENT WAYS.

*Sir Alex Ferguson, 2009*

**THE REAL FRIEND IS
THE ONE WHO WALKS
THROUGH THE DOOR
WHEN THE OTHERS
ARE PUTTING ON THEIR
COATS TO LEAVE.**

*Sir Alex Ferguson, 2009*

# DO NOT COMPARE ME TO THAT WOMAN!

*Journalist foolishly suggests a comparison between Sir Alex and Margaret Thatcher*

# ON
# MANAGEMENT

**THE ONLY ADVICE I
CAN GIVE TO YOU IS
DON'T LET THE PLAYERS
TAKE THE MICKEY
OUT OF YOU.**

*Advice to Paul Ince on being a manager*

# I'VE MELLOWED. I'VE GOT MORE EXPERIENCE. I'VE GOT MORE AUTHORITY. AND THAT'S ALL BECAUSE OF SUCCESS.

*Sir Alex Ferguson, 1999*

# IT'S ABOUT THE TEAM. I CAN GIVE THE LEADERSHIP AND THE DIRECTION BUT THE TEAM HAS TO GEL.

*Sir Alex Ferguson, 2009*

# SOMETIMES YOU HAVE TO FORCE PLAYERS INTO BEING BETTER THAN WHAT THEY THINK THEY ARE.

*Sir Alex Ferguson, 2012*

**I THINK YOU CAN
LEARN SOMETHING
ABOUT YOUR OWN WORLD
FROM ANYONE ELSE'S.
I READ A LOT OF HISTORY
AND IN MOST HISTORY
BOOKS THERE WON'T BE
A MENTION OF SPORT,
BUT THERE ARE ALWAYS
INSIGHTS YOU CAN LEARN.**

*Sir Alex Ferguson, 2009*

PART OF MY JOB IS TO
MAKE SURE THESE LADS
KEEP THEIR FEET ON
THE GROUND. I HAMMER
IT INTO THEM THAT THE
WORK ETHIC IS WHAT
GOT THEM THROUGH
THE DOOR IN THE FIRST
PLACE, AND THEY MUST
NEVER LOSE IT.

*Sir Alex Ferguson, 2009*

# CONTROL.
# MANAGING CHANGE.
# AND OBSERVATION.

*Sir Alex Ferguson on the three qualities
needed for leadership, 2009*

# DON'T EVER THINK YOU'RE ABOVE A CHALLENGE. IT'S NOT RIGHT. ARROGANCE IS NOT A QUALITY, IT'S A HINDRANCE TO SUCCESS.

*Sir Alex Ferguson, 2010*

YOU CAN'T EVER LOSE
CONTROL, NOT WHEN
YOU ARE DEALING WITH 30
TOP PROFESSIONALS WHO
ARE ALL MILLIONAIRES.
IF THEY MISBEHAVE, WE
FINE THEM, BUT WE KEEP
IT INDOORS. AND
IF ANYONE STEPS OUT
OF MY CONTROL,
THAT'S THEM DEAD.

*Sir Alex Ferguson, Harvard interview, 2012*

I REMEMBER GOING TO
SEE ANDREA BOCELLI,
THE OPERA SINGER.
I HAD NEVER BEEN TO
A CLASSICAL CONCERT
IN MY LIFE. BUT I AM
WATCHING THIS AND
THINKING ABOUT THE
CO-ORDINATION AND
THE TEAMWORK.

*Sir Alex Ferguson on seeking
new inspiration, 2012*

I SPEAK TO THE PLAYERS
I'VE LEFT OUT. I DO IT
PRIVATELY. IT'S NOT
EASY, BUT I DO THEM ALL
MYSELF ... I HAVE BEEN
DROPPED FROM A CUP
FINAL IN SCOTLAND AS
A PLAYER AT TEN PAST
TWO, SO I KNOW WHAT
IT FEELS LIKE.

*Sir Alex Ferguson, Harvard interview 2012*

# YOU BASTARD!

*Sir Alex Ferguson on being told by Dunfermline manager Bill Cunningham he wasn't playing in the Scottish Cup Final, 1965*

# TEACUPS AND HAIRDRYERS

# THROWING TEACUPS?
# THAT ONLY HAPPENED
# ONCE OR TWICE.

*Sir Alex Ferguson, 2008*

MYTHS GROW ALL
THE TIME. IF I WAS TO
LISTEN TO THE NUMBER
OF TIMES I'VE THROWN
TEACUPS THEN WE'VE
GONE THROUGH SOME
CROCKERY IN THIS
PLACE. IT'S COMPLETELY
EXAGGERATED.

*Sir Alex Ferguson*

IF A PLAYER ANSWERED
ME BACK, I WOULD HEAD
STRAIGHT FOR THEM,
THIS IS WHERE THE
HAIRDRYER TREATMENT
COMES IN. I DIDN'T
ALLOW A PLAYER
TO BEAT ME IN AN
ARGUMENT.

*Sir Alex Ferguson, 2012*

# THERE'S NOTHING WRONG WITH LOSING YOUR TEMPER, IF IT IS FOR THE RIGHT REASONS.

*Sir Alex Ferguson, 2012*

I CAME IN, THERE WAS
THIS BIG TEA URN AND I
WENT IN TO SMASH IT –
AND I'M NOT KIDDING YOU,
I NEARLY BROKE MY ARM.
I KICKED THE TRAY SO
HARD THE CUPS WENT UP
OVER THE WALL. ARCHIE
KNOX, MY ASSISTANT, WAS
SITTING THERE WITH TEA
RUNNING DOWN THE BACK
OF HIS TRACKSUIT.

*Sir Alex Ferguson, 2008*

# THAT WAS MARK HUGHES WHO INVENTED THAT PHRASE. AFTER HE LEFT ME, OF COURSE.

*Sir Alex Ferguson on the hairdryer, 2008*

# WHERE'S F**KING BARNES?

*Sir Alex Ferguson on the warpath after losing to
Wimbledon, 1986. Winger Peter Barnes was
hiding in an ice cold bath to avoid him*

# I SAT THERE. I TOOK THE HAIRDRYER ON THE CHIN, IN MY FACE, IN MY EYES, EVERYTHING CAME OUT OF HIS MOUTH. HE SPAT AT ME. HE SHOUTED AT ME. I WENT OUT IN THE SECOND HALF AND SCORED.

*Dion Dublin on getting the hairdryer treatment*

I DID THINK IT WAS
WEIRD, THE FIRST TIME
HE ATTACKED PAUL
MCGRATH WITH THE
HAIRDRYER. YOU JUST
HAD TO HIDE YOUR
HEAD BECAUSE YOU'D
START LAUGHING THAT
IT WASN'T YOU.

*Bryan Robson on the hairdryer treatment*

# I'M A PUSSYCAT NOW, TOO OLD TO LOSE MY TEMPER.

*Sir Alex Ferguson, 2008*

# ARSENE
# WENGER

# HE'S A NOVICE.
# HE SHOULD KEEP
# HIS OPINIONS TO
# JAPANESE FOOTBALL.

*An opening salvo on Arsene Wenger, 1996*

# HE'S AT A BIG CLUB, WELL, THEY USED TO BE A BIG CLUB ... HE SHOULD KEEP HIS MOUTH SHUT, FIRMLY SHUT.

*On Arsene Wenger, 1997*

**THEY SAY HE'S AN INTELLIGENT MAN, RIGHT? SPEAKS FIVE LANGUAGES! I'VE GOT A FIFTEEN-YEAR-OLD BOY FROM THE IVORY COAST WHO SPEAKS FIVE LANGUAGES.**

*On Arsene Wenger, 2003*

# IT'S GETTING TICKLY NOW – SQUEAKY-BUM TIME, I CALL IT.

*Sir Alex's coins his now legendary phrase during the 2003 title run-in against Arsenal*

IN THE TUNNEL WENGER
WAS CRITICISING MY
PLAYERS, CALLING THEM
CHEATS, SO I TOLD HIM
TO LEAVE THEM ALONE
AND BEHAVE HIMSELF.
HE RAN AT ME WITH
HIS HANDS RAISED
SAYING 'WHAT DO YOU
WANT TO DO ABOUT
IT?' TO NOT APOLOGISE

FOR THE BEHAVIOUR
OF THE PLAYERS TO
ANOTHER MANAGER IS
UNTHINKABLE. IT'S A
DISGRACE, BUT I DON'T
EXPECT WENGER TO
EVER APOLOGISE, HE'S
THAT TYPE OF PERSON.

*After the 'Battle of the Buffet'*
*at Arsenal, 2005*

# EVERYONE THINKS THEY HAVE THE PRETTIEST WIFE AT HOME.

*Arsene Wenger, on Sir Alex's suggestion that Manchester United played more attractive football than Arsenal.*

# LIVERPOOL

# A LOT OF MANAGERS HAVE TO LEAVE HERE CHOKING ON THEIR OWN SICK, BITING THEIR TONGUE, AFRAID TO TELL THE TRUTH.

*Furious about refereeing decisions at Anfield after a 3-3 draw, 1988*

# YOU MIGHT AS WELL TALK TO MY DAUGHTER, YOU'LL GET MORE SENSE OUR OF HER.

*Kenny Dalglish offers his baby daughter
Lauren to respond to Sir Alex's claims
of referee bias at Anfield, 1988*

# I THINK HE WAS AN ANGRY MAN. HE MUST HAVE BEEN DISTURBED FOR SOME REASON. I THINK YOU HAVE GOT TO CUT THROUGH THE VENOM OF IT AND HOPEFULLY HE'LL REFLECT AND UNDERSTAND WHAT HE SAID WAS ABSOLUTELY RIDICULOUS.

*Sir Alex's reaction to Rafael Benítez's*
*infamous 'facts' rant, 2009*

**WEIRD. I REALLY DON'T KNOW WHAT HE WAS TALKING ABOUT. HE'D OBVIOUSLY WORKED HIMSELF UP INTO SOMETHING, BECAUSE HE WAS READING IT OUT.**

*Sir Alex Ferguson on the Benitez 'facts' rant again*

# I WOULD NEED TO READ MORE OF FREUD BEFORE I COULD REALLY UNDERSTAND ALL THAT.

*More reaction to the 'facts' rant*

# NOW YOU KNOW, IT'S US AGAINST THE WORLD BOYS.

*Sir Alex Ferguson to the team after losing at Liverpool, ending their chances of winning the 1991/92. The Liverpool fans had asked for the players' autographs and torn them up in front of them*

# MY GREATEST CHALLENGE IS NOT WHAT'S HAPPENING AT THE MOMENT, MY GREATEST CHALLENGE WAS KNOCKING LIVERPOOL OFF THEIR F**KING PERCH.

*Sir Alex on the 2002/03 title race*

# MIND GAMES

**WHEN WE WON THE LEAGUE I CAME OUT OF THE DRESSING ROOM AND I SAID, 'I'VE WRITTEN THREE NAMES PUT THEM IN AN ENVELOPE – THOSE ARE THE THREE PLAYERS WHO ARE GOING TO LET US DOWN NEXT SEASON.'**

*Mind games with his new
Premiership champions, 1993*

**BLACKBURN WILL
HAVE TO FINISH LIKE
DEVON LOCH TO GIVE
US ANY CHANCE.**

*Sir Alex on the 1994/95 title race*

# WHEN YOUR FORM GOES AT THIS LATE STAGE OF THE SEASON, YOU CAN'T DO ANYTHING ABOUT IT ... THE FACT WE ARE NOW JUST TWO POINTS BEHIND THEM IS ALSO GOING TO MAKE IT ALL THE HARDER PSYCHOLOGICALLY.

*Sir Alex offers Blackburn some helpful advice in the 1994/95 title race*

# I COULD NOT BE WHOLLY SATISFIED WITH WINNING THE PREMIERSHIP IF MY TEAM HAD PLAYED LIKE BLACKBURN ROVERS THIS SEASON.

*Ferguson on Blackburn, who beat Manchester United to the 1994/95 title*

**THEY RAISED THEIR
GAME BECAUSE
THEY WERE PLAYING
MANCHESTER UNITED. IT
WAS PATHETIC. I THINK
WE CAN ACCEPT ANY
CLUB COMING HERE AND
TRYING THEIR HARDEST
SO LONG AS THEY DO
IT EVERY WEEK.**

*Sir Alex on Leeds United, whose next opponents
were Keegan's Newcastle, 1996*

I'LL TELL YOU SOMETHING, HE WENT DOWN IN MY ESTIMATION WHEN HE SAID THAT. WE HAVE NOT RESORTED TO THAT. BUT I'LL TELL HIM NOW IF HE'S WATCHING IT. WE'RE STILL FIGHTING FOR THIS TITLE ... AND I'LL TELL YOU SOMETHING – I WILL LOVE IT IF WE BEAT THEM, LOVE IT.

*Kevin Keegan responds to the mind games
live on Sky, 1996*

# FERGUSON AGAINST THE REST OF THE WORLD

# YOU SCUMBAG,
# YOU RATBAG,
# YOU DIRTY BASTARD!

*Sir Alex Ferguson let's Feyenoord's
Paul Bosvelt knows what he thinks
of his tackle on Denis Irwin, 1997*

# I WOULD NOT
# SELL THEM A VIRUS.

*Sir Alex's reaction to the question was he selling*
*Cristiano Ronaldo to Real Madrid, 2008*

I READ THAT SCOLARI IS MORE EXPERIENCED THAN ME. WHAT HAVE I BEEN DOING FOR THE LAST 34 YEARS? I MUST HAVE MISSED SOMETHING OR BEEN ASLEEP SOMEWHERE.

*Taking Big Phil down a notch at Chelsea, 2008*

# I ALWAYS REMEMBER THE LOCAL MP COMPLAINING ABOUT IT IN THE HOUSE OF COMMONS. HE SAID THE POTTERIES PUBLIC WERE BEING DENIED THE CHANCE TO SEE GREAT PLAYERS.

*Parliamentary questions about Sir Alex picking 'kids' for a 1994 League Cup tie v Port Vale. The 'kids' in question were David Beckham, Paul Scholes, Gary Neville and Nicky Butt*

# WE WILL NOT LET THIS
# MAN DENY US THE TITLE.

*On referee David Elleray sending
Denis Irwin off against Liverpool, 1999*

# THEY GOT HIM SENT OFF, EVERYONE SPRINTED TOWARDS THE REFEREE, TYPICAL GERMANS.

*On Rafael's sending against Bayern Munich in the 2010 Champions League*

**WHEN AN ITALIAN SAYS IT'S PASTA I CHECK UNDER THE SAUCE TO MAKE SURE. THEY ARE INNOVATORS OF THE SMOKESCREEN.**

*Sir Alex before playing Inter Milan, 1999*

# ALEX ACTED WITHIN HOURS. IT WAS LIKE FOUR TYRES BEING PUNCTURED ON THE SAME CAR.

*Preston chairman Maurice Lindsay sacks Sir Alex's son Darren as manager; Sir Alex recalls his Manchester United loanees in response*

**JOSE IS VERY
INTELLIGENT, HE HAS
CHARISMA, HIS PLAYERS
PLAY FOR HIM, AND HE IS
A GOOD LOOKING GUY.
I THINK I HAVE MOST
OF THOSE THINGS,
TOO, APART FROM
HIS GOOD LOOKS.**

*On José Mourinho, talk to
Harvard Students 2012*

# NOISY
# NEIGHBOURS

# THEY ARE A SMALL CLUB, WITH A SMALL MENTALITY. ALL THEY CAN TALK ABOUT IS MANCHESTER UNITED.

*On Manchester City, 2009*

SOMETIMES YOU HAVE A
NOISY NEIGHBOUR. YOU
CANNOT DO ANYTHING
ABOUT THAT. THEY WILL
ALWAYS BE NOISY. YOU
JUST HAVE TO GET ON
WITH YOUR LIFE, PUT
YOUR TELEVISION ON
AND TURN IT UP A
BIT LOUDER.

*On Manchester City, 2009*

THEY COULD BUY EVERY PLAYER IN THE WORLD, BUT CAN THEY BUY A TEAM, CAN THEY BUY A MANCHESTER UNITED SPIRIT? ... THE PROBLEM WITH ALL THAT MONEY IS THAT YOU BUY INDISCRIMINATELY.

# SUNDERLAND IN THE 1950S, THE BANK OF ENGLAND TEAM; RELEGATED.

*Sir Alex Ferguson on Manchester City, 2010*

# MEDIA
# RELATIONS

# ON YOU GO. I'M NO F\*\*KING TALKING TO YOU. HE'S A F\*\*KING GREAT PLAYER. YOUS ARE F\*\*KING IDIOTS.

*Losing it in a press conference over criticisms of Juan Sebastián Verón, 2002*

**HAVE YOU SEEN OUR FIXTURES LIST? IF YOU HAD, YOU WOULDN'T EVEN ASK THAT QUESTION. YOU HAVE NO IDEA. NO IDEA AT ALL. THAT'S IT, IT'S ALL OVER. YOU CAN ALL F\*\*K OFF, THE LOT OF YOU.**

*Sir Alex Ferguson asked at a press conference why he couldn't field a youth team in the FA Cup, rather than withdrawing to play in the World Club Competition, 1999*

SOME OF THE EX-
PLAYER, EX-MANAGER
PUNDITS ARE THE
WORST. IT'S A DISGRACE
THE WAY THEY SIT
THERE CRITICISING GUYS
THEY USED TO PLAY
WITH, JUST TO MAKE
A BIT OF IMPACT.

*Sir Alex Ferguson, 2009*

# YOU WANT A F\*\*KING STORY AS USUAL ... YOUR F\*\*KING STUFF IS A DISGRACE TO JOURNALISM AND YOU ARE. THE STUFF YOU F\*\*KING COME OUT WITH ...

*Sir Alex Ferguson takes a tabloid journalist to task, 2002*

# I DON'T KNOW WHAT YOU'RE TALKING ABOUT. I THINK THAT'LL DO US THERE.

*A brave talkSPORT journalist asks Sir Alex Ferguson that if he puts the fear of God into players, what scares him, 2009*

# FERGUSON
# AND THE BBC

JIMMY HILL IS VERBAL WHEN IT SUITS HIM. IF THERE'S A PRAT GOING ABOUT IN THIS WORLD, HE IS THE PRAT. HE WRITES US OFF IN THE WARM-UP, THAT'S HOW MUCH HE KNOWS ABOUT THE GAME.

*Sir Alex Ferguson after Jimmy Hill had criticised Eric Cantona, 1994*

**THE BBC ARE DYING FOR US TO LOSE. EVERYONE IS FROM LIVERPOOL WITH A SUPPORTER'S BADGE. THEY WILL BE AT OUR GAMES EVERY WEEK UNTIL WE LOSE, THAT MOB, BOB, BARRY, HANSEN – THE LOT OF THEM.**

*Sir Alex Ferguson on the BBC, 1994*

YOU'VE NO RIGHT TO
ASK ME THAT QUESTION
JOHN. YOU'RE OUT OF
ORDER ... YOU KNOW
FINE WELL MY RULING
ON THAT. RIGHT,
THAT'S THE INTERVIEW
FINISHED ... I'M GOING
TO CANCEL THAT
INTERVIEW, THE WHOLE
F**KING LOT OF IT.

# CANCEL IT, RIGHT?
# F**KING MAKE SURE
# THAT DOES NOT
# GO OUT, JOHN.

*John Motson gets the hairdryer treatment after
asking a question Ferguson doesn't like, 1995*

# WHAT I'M DOING WITH THE BBC ISN'T A GRUDGE. IT'S A STANCE.

*On BBC dispute, 2008*

# PLAYERS

IF HE WAS AN INCH
TALLER HE'D BE THE
BEST CENTRE-HALF IN
BRITAIN. HIS FATHER IS
6FT 2IN – I'D CHECK
THE MILKMAN.

*On Gary Neville*

I REMEMBER THE
FIRST TIME I SAW HIM.
HE WAS 13 AND JUST
FLOATED OVER THE
GROUND LIKE A COCKER
SPANIEL CHASING A
PIECE OF SILVER PAPER
IN THE WIND.

*On Ryan Giggs*

# THAT LAD MUST HAVE BEEN BORN OFFSIDE.

*On Filippo Inzaghi*

# HE COULD START A ROW
# IN AN EMPTY HOUSE.

*On Dennis Wise*

IT WAS AN INCIDENT
WHICH WAS FREAKISH.
IF I TRIED IT A HUNDRED
OR A MILLION TIMES IT
COULD NOT HAPPEN
AGAIN. IF I COULD,
I WOULD HAVE
CARRIED ON PLAYING.

*On the David Beckham boot incident, 2003*

# YOU KNOW, HE TRIED IT ABOUT TEN MINUTES BEFORE HE SCORED AND I SAID TO MY ASSISTANT BRIAN KIDD, 'IF HE TRIES THAT AGAIN, HE'S OFF'.

*On the Beckham wondergoal, 2008*

**HIS LIFE CHANGED
WHEN HE MET HIS WIFE.
SHE'S IN POP AND DAVID
GOT ANOTHER IMAGE.
HE'D DEVELOPED THIS
'FASHION THING'.**

*Sir Alex on Victoria Beckham's
influence on her husband, 2003*

# HE LOOKED LIKE A MANCHESTER UNITED PLAYER AS SOON AS I SAW HIM.

*Sir Alex Ferguson on Roy Keane, 1999*

# IF THERE WAS EVER A PLAYER IN THIS WORLD WHO WAS MADE FOR MANCHESTER UNITED, IT WAS CANTONA.

*Sir Alex Ferguson, 2008*

**COURAGE IN FOOTBALL, AS IN LIFE, COMES IN MANY FORMS. THE COURAGE TO CONTINUE, NO MATTER HOW MANY TIMES HE IS GOING TO BE KICKED, IDENTIFIES RONALDO.**

*Sir Alex Ferguson, 2008*

# LETTING GO OF JAAP STAM. NO QUESTION.

*Sir Alex Ferguson on his biggest mistake, 2009*

# NOT GETTING GAZZA. HE WAS A FABULOUS FOOTBALLER AND HE WOULD HAVE DONE BRILLIANTLY HERE.

*Sir Alex Ferguson on his biggest disappointment, 2009*

# HE'S A ONE-OFF IN TERMS OF THE MODERN TYPE OF FRAGILE PLAYER WE'RE GETTING TODAY, COCOONED BY THEIR AGENTS, MOTHERS AND FATHERS, PSYCHOLOGISTS, WELFARE OFFICERS ... HE'S A THROWBACK.

*Sir Alex Ferguson on Wayne Rooney, 2010*

# I GOT A TEXT FROM HIM LAST WEEK SAYING 'I MISS YOU SO MUCH'. I'D TEXTED HIM TO SAY HAPPY BIRTHDAY.

*Sir Alex Ferguson on Ronaldo, 2010*

**HE SAID, 'GARTH CROOKS AND I HAVE AN UNDERSTANDING.' I SAID, 'HAVE YOU? AYE, IT'S A GOOD ONE. HE'S SCORING GOALS AND YOU'RE MESSING AROUND IN THE MIDDLE OF THE PARK.'**

*Sir Alex remembering giving
Steve Archibald it straight, 2010*

# I CAN JUST IMAGINE HIM NOW, SITTING AT HIS DESK WITH A MAP OF GREATER MANCHESTER, PLOTTING OUR DRINKING ROUTE, PUTTING IN PINS WHEREVER WE'VE BEEN SPOTTED.

*Paul McGrath,* News of the World *interview on leaving Manchester United*

# YOU AND WILLIE MILLER ARE BLEEDING THE CLUB DRY. I'LL GIVE YOU ANOTHER FIVER A WEEK.

*Alex McLeish attempts and fails to leave*
*Aberdeen for Tottenham, 1984*

WE GOT A GREAT PIECE
OF LUCK WHEN WE
TOOK RYAN GIGGS FROM
MANCHESTER CITY ...
WE WERE UP AT RYAN'S
DOOR EVERY NIGHT
UNTIL HE SIGNED.

*Sir Alex Ferguson*

# IT WAS ANIMAL INSTINCT. I SMELLED DANGER AFTER THE FIRST WEMBLEY GAME. I KNEW JIM HAD TO BE DROPPED.

*Replacing Jim Leighton with Les Sealey
for the 1990 FA Cup Final replay*

# SOMETIMES YOU LOOK IN A FIELD AND YOU SEE A COW AND THINK IT'S A BETTER COW THAN THE ONE YOU'VE GOT IN YOUR OWN FIELD. IT NEVER REALLY WORKS OUT THAT WAY.

*Sir Alex on Wayne Rooney asking for a transfer*

# HE'S A F**KING
# BIG-TIME CHARLIE.

*Sir Alex on Paul Ince, 1998*

# I OPENED SHARPEY'S DOOR. I WAS HOLDING A BECKS AND THERE WAS NO ESCAPE.

*Ryan Giggs on being caught red-handed in party mode by Sir Alex Ferguson*

OF ALL THE MANY
QUALITIES A GOOD
TEAM MUST POSSESS,
THE SUPREME ESSENTIAL
FOR ME IS PENETRATION.
AND ERIC BROUGHT
THE CAN-OPENER.

*On Eric Cantona*

# IF I WAS PUTTING ROY KEANE OUT THERE TO REPRESENT MANCHESTER UNITED ON A ONE AGAINST ONE, WE'D WIN THE DERBY, THE NATIONAL, THE BOAT RACE AND ANYTHING ELSE.

*On Roy Keane*

# WINNING THE CHAMPIONS LEAGUE

# DEEP DOWN, I KNOW IT WOULD BE IMPOSSIBLE TO WIN THE LEAGUE, THE CHAMPIONS' CUP AND THE FA CUP.

*Sir Alex Ferguson, 1997*

**IF YOU LOSE, YOU'LL GO UP TO COLLECT LOSERS' MEDALS AND YOU'LL BE SIX FEET AWAY FROM THE EUROPEAN CUP. BUT YOU WON'T BE ABLE TO TOUCH IT.**

*Sir Alex Ferguson's half time team talk,*
*European Cup Final 1999*

# CAN YOU F**KING
# BELIEVE HIM!

*On Peter Schmeichel as he went up for the*
*stoppage time corner in Barcelona, 1999*

# I CAN'T BELIEVE IT.
# I CAN'T BELIEVE IT.
# FOOTBALL,
# BLOODY HELL.

*His now famous post-match interview after
the Champions League victory in 1999*

# ON
# FERGUSON

I HONESTLY THINK HE WOULD GET UP IN THE MIDDLE OF THE NIGHT AND GO 300 MILES IN THE CAR IF HE THOUGHT THERE WAS A PLAYER WORTH WATCHING, SOMEONE HE COULD SIGN FOR THE CLUB.

*Sir Bobby Charlton*

THAT WAS THE ONE THING
ABOUT THE BOSS; IF WE
WERE DRAWING HE WAS
NOT HAPPY AND WOULD
MAKE A CHANGE TO TRY
AND WIN THE GAME. HE
WOULD NEVER SETTLE FOR
A POINT AND BECAUSE OF
THAT THE UNITED FANS
HAVE BECOME USED
TO WINNING.

*Bryan Robson*

**A FATHER FIGURE TO
ME FROM THE MOMENT
I ARRIVED AT THE CLUB
AT THE AGE OF 11 UNTIL
THE DAY I LEFT.**

*David Beckham*

# THAT WAS NOT A FOOTBALL TEAM WE MET. IT WAS AN UNSTOPPABLE SPIRIT.

*Alfredo Di Stéfano, manager of Real Madrid, beaten by Ferguson's Aberdeen in the 1983 Cup Winners' Cup Final*

# THIS IS ONLY THE START. HAVE YOU SEEN THEIR YOUTH TEAM?

*David Pleat on Manchester United, 1992*

# DON'T YOU THINK HE'S WON ENOUGH ALREADY?

*Cathy Ferguson, on being asked by Alastair Campbell about her husband being knighted*

# ON FOOTBALL

# FOOTBALL IS LIKE
# A DRUG WHICH IS
# DIFFICULT TO GIVE UP.

*Sir Alex Ferguson, 2008*

# WINNING A TROPHY DOESN'T REALLY MEAN ANYTHING TO ME AFTER IT'S GONE. AT THE TIME IT'S THE MOST TREASURED THING. BUT AS SOON AS IT'S OVER, IT'S SOON FORGOTTEN.

*Sir Alex Ferguson, 1999*

**FOOTBALL IS A HARD GAME; THERE'S NO DENYING IT. IT'S A GAME THAT CAN BRING OUT THE WORST IN YOU.**

*Sir Alex Ferguson, 2008*

**THE LIST OF GENTLE, NATURALLY RETIRING MEN WHO HAVE BEEN SUCCESSFUL IN THEIR ATTEMPTS AT RUNNING CLUBS ISN'T A LONG ONE, IS IT?**

*Sir Alex Ferguson, 2008*

# PELE, DI STEFANO, MARADONA, CRUYFF.

*Sir Alex Ferguson on the best players he ever saw, 2009*

**WHEN I WENT TO
RANGERS, THE THOUGHT
IN MY MIND WAS,
'I AM GOING TO WIN
SOMETHING HERE ...'
I DIDN'T WIN A SAUSAGE.**

*Sir Alex Ferguson, 2008*

**PLAYERS THESE DAYS
HAVE LIVED MORE
SHELTERED LIVES, SO
THEY ARE MUCH MORE
FRAGILE NOW THAN
25 YEARS AGO.**

*Sir Alex Ferguson, 2012*

# THE WORST CRIME IN THE GAME. IT'S A COWARD'S WAY OF PLAYING.

*On the use of elbows, 2002*

# THE END

# RETIREMENT IS FOR YOUNG PEOPLE

*Sir Alex Ferguson*

# EVERY SINGLE ONE OF US LOVES ALEX FERGUSON.

*On news of Alex Ferguson saying he was retiring in 2001, United fans chanted this for 31 minutes during the match against Spurs*

# I WILL BE LEAVING
# MANCHESTER UNITED
# AT THE END OF THE
# SEASON AND THAT IS IT.

*Sir Alex Ferguson, adamant in 2002*

# WE'VE DECIDED YOU'RE NOT RETIRING.

*Cathy Ferguson and her sons have a quiet family chat with Sir Alex, 2002*

# EVERY SINGLE ONE OF US LOVES CATHY FERGUSON.

*United fans on the news Sir Alex had decided
not to retire after all, chanting during
match against Charlton, 2002*

# IT WAS IMPORTANT TO ME TO LEAVE AN ORGANISATION IN THE STRONGEST POSSIBLE SHAPE AND I BELIEVE I HAVE DONE SO.

*Sir Alex Ferguson, announces his retirement, 8 May 2013*

# TO THE FANS, THANK YOU. IT HAS BEEN AN HONOUR AND AN ENORMOUS PRIVILEGE.

*Sir Alex Ferguson, announces his retirement, 8 May 2013*

# I DON'T KNOW HOW WE ARE GOING TO MOVE FORWARD. I'M 28, THAT'S ALL I'VE KNOW ALL MY LIFE – FERGIE. MY BOSS SENT ME HOME, I'M THAT BAD.

*Troubled fan on radio phone-in, the day*
*Sir Alex announced his retirement*

# TWENTY-THREE YEARS OF SILVER AND WE'RE STILL TOP. TA-RA FERGIE

*Banner at Old Trafford, 12 May 2013*